A Guide to the Planning of Educational Facilities

Third Edition

Dr. John H. Holcomb

UNIVERSITY
PRESS OF
AMERICA

Lanham • New York • London

Copyright © 1995 by
University Press of America,® Inc.
4720 Boston Way
Lanham, Maryland 20706

3 Henrietta Street
London WC2E 8LU England

Library of Congress Cataloging-in-Publication Data
Holcomb, John H.
A guide to the planning of educational facilities / John H. Holcomb.
— 3rd ed.
p.   cm.
Includes bibliographical references and index.
1. School buildings. 2. School facilities—Planning. I. Title.
LB3205.H65   1994   371.62—dc20   94–38334 CIP

ISBN 0–8191–9785–8 (cloth : alk. paper)
ISBN 0–8191–9786–6 (pbk. : alk. paper)

Contents

Introduction

The building program of a school district is one of the most important activities in which a board of education, local administration, faculty, and the citizens of the district can become involved. The building program requires large sums of money and has a direct bearing on both the quantity and quality of the educational program to be offered the children of that district.

Decisions regarding building programs are generally irrevocable, especially once the program reaches the construction phase. One of the most difficult aspects of the program and one which causes many board members and administrators to be reluctant to enter a building program is that each new decision is based on previous decisions. Future planning, construction and curricular programs are based on prior decisions made regarding the physical aspects of the building.

The trauma of making these final-type decisions has prompted many boards of education and their school administrators into delaying building commitments until the district is forced into a hastily-conceived and ill-planned program of construction expedience.

The results of this kind of building program are seldom satisfactory, but are often justified by stating, "We had to have the schools in a hurry." This may be true in some instances, but usually the crisis has developed because the hard decisions regarding school expansion was delayed . . . and delayed . . . and delayed, until a real emergency develops.

Most communities will go through eight general phases during a school construction project. The phases, as identified here, are not necessarily all-inclusive. They will also involve considerable overlap, but they should be fairly representative in aiding your building processes. These steps include:

1. The Thinking and Needs Assessment Phase.
2. The Planning and Commitment Phase.
3. The Design Phase.
4. The "Selling" Phase.
5. The Financing Phase.
6. The Construction Phase.
7. The Occupation and In-Service Orientation Phase.
8. The Evaluation Phase

The author has added a "Chapter 9" dealing with educational facilities remodeling and renovation. This approach to the development of adequate educational facilities if becoming more popular, as the tax dollars for education continue to dwindle.

The purpose of this booklet is to provide both information and assistance to local school districts during the planning and the development process of a school building program. The information contained here represents both the author's professional judgments and ideas from many selected sources as gained by the author during his 30 years of experience as a public school administrator.

However, it will be the responsibility of each school district and its respective community to assess additional local needs and plan adequately for the future. It is a tough job, but, with good planning and community support and involvement, can be one of the most rewarding aspects of school boardsmanship.

Best of luck,

Dr. John H. Holcomb, Professor
Educational Administration

Chapter 1

The Thinking and
Needs Assessment Phase

The need for a school construction program usually becomes apparent first to one of the school administrators, either the superintendent or one of the building principals. The administrator is usually led to this observation when he finds he has more students or teachers to schedule than he has space to accommodate, or when repair or maintenance problems become so numerous that the economic-educational worth of the building is questionable. The most obvious answer to inadequate space requirements is building additional space.

But, before the administrator proposes this to his board of education and to the community, he should be prepared to answer at least the following questions:

1. Is there a way to utilize more effectively space currently available?
2. Would different space-time patterns relieve the need for additional facilities? If so, what are these space-time alternatives and would they be acceptable to the students, patrons, and staff?

3. Is the student population increasing and if so, at what rate?
4. Does any other group (staff, board, community) recognize that there is a need for additional space?
5. Are existing buildings becoming obsolete or in such a state of disrepair that renovation is not practical?
6. Is there a change in the community's population pattern? Are more young families moving into the community? Is there new industry?
7. Has there been a change, or is a change anticipated in land usage, particularly where it might be moving from rural and agrarian, to urban, industrial or residential?

It is important that the board and administration generally agree on the answers to the above questions before they proceed further into a building program. This will prevent a number of "second-guessing" problems as the building program develops.

It is important to remember that the physical plant is only built to house an educational program; IT MUST NOT BECOME AN END IN ITSELF. Therefore, at this early stage of planning, the board, professional educators and community members should start preliminary planning for the educational specifications to be developed. (The development of the educational specifications will be discussed in more detail later in this publication.)

Community Involvement

The American public school system has depended on its citizenry for moral support and interest as well as direction and funding. The support that the people can give their local schools depends on how well they understand the problems and intent of those schools. Usually, we equate this support with help in curriculum development, but it is no less important as a school district develops a building program.

Early in any anticipated construction program, the board of education should appoint a group of lay citizens to assist in reaching decisions on certain aspect of proposed construction. This committee can function under any one of several different titles, including "blue ribbon planning committee", "lay advisory committee", and "citizen's committee". Regardless of the title, the function remains very much the same.

It is important that as soon as the advisory committee is appointed it be charged by either the superintendent or a member of the school board (preferably the board president) as to the *advisory* role it is to play. The charge should set forth clearly the duties of the committee, the expectations of the board in relation to the work of the committee, a suggested time-table, and the resources the board will make available to the committee; visits to other districts, clerical or secretarial assistance, consultant fees, etc.

Nothing is more discouraging to a group of citizens than to assume it is in a policy-making role when actually it is simply being asked for its advice.

This committee can assist in a building program in a number of ways. It can conduct surveys of existing school buildings, make utilization studies, make visitations to other districts, make recommendations for design and student usage, recommend whether an existing building is to be replaced or remodeled, and assist in the design of the community use of any new or remodeled construction.

Some guidelines in the development of citizen committees are valuable to prevent hard feeling and and misunderstanding. Committees that are effective have certain common characteristics:

1. The committee is broadly representative of the community, including geographic, as well as occupational, cultural, economic and political representation.

2. It gathers facts, seeks descriptive information and bases its recommendations on all available, relevant information.

3. The board of education adopts a written statement of purpose for the committee, focusing on specific problems and setting deadlines for the committee. These deadlines are for interim reports as well as a final, summary recommendation report.

4. The various levels of the school administration are informed as to the functions and roles of the committee to assure cooperation and support as the committee does its job.

5. Lines of communication between the advisory committee and the mass media are outlined. This prevents individual members of the committee from making "off the record" remarks to members of the mass media, or to members of the community.

6. Adequate time is spent with the committee to plan for the work it is expected to do. In order to provide for this groundwork, the background and the need for the study must be clearly explained to members of the committee as well as the nature and scope of the recommendation(s) they are expected to make.

7. An outline for committee operation delineates the limits of the committee's authority, prescribes the reporting deadlines, and defines the way in which reports are to be made to the board, public, school administration, and others interested in the project.

Developing the Time Table

It is also important that everyone involved with the building program realize that schools cannot be developed overnight. After the committees are formed, the following time-table might be used as a basis for planning, depending on local conditions and the size and complexity of the school to be built:

1. Basic analysis of building needs including:
   a. Evaluation of existing plant facilities.
   b. Pupil enrollment projections.
   c. Determination of instructional program and methodology.
   d. Analysis of financial ability.
   e. Impact of school site selection on total community.
   f. Selection of architect   3 Months

2. Development of Educational Specifications   3 Months
3. Selection of Site   2 Months
4. Development of Schematic Plans   3 Months
5. Approval of plans by State Education Agency   1 Month
6. Development of working drawings and
   specifications   6 Months
7. Board and staff review   2 Months
8. Final drawings and specifications   1 Month
9. Final approval from State Education Agency
   and obtaining permits   1 Month
10. Advertising, bidding, and awarding of
    contracts   2 Months
11. Site development, construction, and
    occupation   12-24 Months

         Total Time Involved   36-48 Months

The times mentioned are estimates based on the experience of many districts. They are subject to numerous variables; scope of the program, the number and experience of the persons responsible for decisions at the various steps, the time of year when bids are let, the available labor and material supply, and financing available for the project. The architect might also suggest time-saving methods, such as "fast-tracking" and "design-build" techniques.

Chapter 2

The Planning and Commitment Phase

At this point the concerns discussed in Chapter 1 are refined into actual building and space needs. It is also during this phase that the administration, the board, and the community make the commitment to the acquisition of more space for their schools. This acquisition of space usually comes in the form of new construction.

It is important at this point that the board, administration, and community ask these basic questions: To what extent do the existing facilities meet the needs of the *desired* educational programs? If the facilities fall short of these needs, is it practical to renovate or enlarge them, or must additional facilities be built? Once these questions are resolved, there are some other important considerations which must be made during this phase in the building program:

1. Do we build modular or "stick-built" facilities?

Will the more traditional type of construction be the acceptable method or do we consider the use of mobile or semi-portable classroom space, prefabricated construction, mobile home-type classroom facilities? Is it better to move classrooms than move students?

2. How long do we anticipate we will use this facility and by whom will it be used?

The answer to these questions may very well have a strong influence on how the previous question is answered. There may be a need to establish temporary facilities, for example, at a temporary mobile home park or a small school facility near a housing project before it is large enough to require a full-sized school. The "instant school" concept is becoming popular as districts find that though the use of portable building they can shift temporary classroom building space throughout the district. They are able to place classrooms on a temporary basis until they can ascertain whether or not a permanent school is needed in that location.

3. What kind of educational program will be put into the new facility; traditional or flexible, elementary or secondary, academic or vocational?

During these times of educational change it would seem of questionable value to build a new facility without the flexibility to provide for the many new techniques and methodology currently entering into educational practices, particularly the advent of the computer. At the same time, a district must provide for the more traditional educational programs which will be in effect well into the next century.

4. What is the best way of financing the new facility?

Does the district have the capability of considering a pay-as-you-go plan or must long range indebtedness be incurred through a bonding process? Very few districts have the capability of paying cash for a new school of any size. Is "lease-purchase" feasible? The state education agency's legal department should be checked for the legality of that possibility. The local administration and community should be charged by the board with exploring the various alternatives available and presenting those alternatives with a recommendation to the board.

5. What is the anticipated enrollment trend in the attendance area to be served by the new school?

Is there a growth area which will continue to provide children for many years to come, or is it an area which has become saturated with families above the child-rearing age? In the saturated population areas, as the students from that area get older, they are not replaced by younger students. Therefore, students from the schools in these areas are eventually bussed to other schools or students from other attendance areas are bussed into that school. In either case, there may be a great deal of dissatisfaction because of the loss of the neighborhood-school concept.

6. What are the best criteria for selecting an architect?

While the actual selection of the architect will be discussed in Chapter 3, there are some basic criteria which the board and administration should consider during this planning and commitment phase. A strong recommendation would be that any board considering a building program visit the state education agency to review plans by various architects on file in that office. State education agencies encourage the examination of several plans which are immediately available and are on file in that office.

Reviewing these plans serves two purposes: (1) It will allow board members and administrators to see what kind of educational construction is current; and (2) It will allow identification of architects involved in the development of these different kinds of plans. The selection of the architect will be discussed at greater length in Chapter 3.

7. Who writes the educational specifications and when are these done?

The details of educational specifications will be discussed later in this publication. However, the board, administration, staff, and community should, at this stage in the development of the building program, make a commitment to the development of educational specifications. Any good school is unique. It is designed to meet the needs of a particular group of students who will be housed, educated, and fed within that particular school.

This modern school will reflect, both in physical design and in educational program, the values, interests, and educational aspirations of the community it serves. Therefore, it is the intent of the educational specifications to set down the desired educational program, present and future. This permits the architect to effectively translate the planned learning activities and the educational philosophy of the district into a brick, glass, steel, and wood structure designed around this educational system. This will also allow those who are responsible to the public to have a ready guide to the educational program which will be housed by the school building.

8. How do we develop a "System of Plans?"

As the anticipated program for the new facility is developed, it is important that a companion and supporting "system of plans" be developed for the following:

A. The Curriculum Plan

This plan will state in writing and in broad terms the desired learning outcomes expected during the lifetime of the school building. It expands and clarifies the school's mission by stating what knowledge, understanding, attitudes, and habits of life should be developed in the experiences of the children while attending that school.

B. The Operations Plan

This plan should set the ground rules for the management of people in the school situation. It will say who is doing what, with whom, and where they are to do this.

C. The Instructional Plan

This describes in as much depth as possible the desired learning outcomes across all areas of the school's responsibility, both academic and non-academic, and will describe what actually takes place in the reaction, interaction, self-learning activities while students and teachers are in school. This plan should terminate with a listing of the courses or specific learning activities to be offered by that school and should define which are elective and which are required.

D. The Organizational Plan

This plan is concerned with which pattern or system is to be adopted to provide for educational and instructional program. Within this plan the following questions will be answered:

1. What will be the grade organization of the school? K-6, 7-12, etc.
2. Is the plan for self-contained classrooms, team teaching, departmentalization, etc?
3. Is it to be ungraded, non-graded, closely graded, etc?
4. What shall be the maximum or minimum numbers of pupils per class? Per instructional area?
5. What is the maximum enrollment acceptable in this building or on this campus?
6. Will there be an open or closed campus lunch program?
7. Will the school library serve only students or will it also serve the public?
8. Will other parts of the building be open to the public, while the rest of the building is secured?

E. The Personnel Plan

This plan, to be developed by the central office, describes the staff activities requirements for the facility. It is here that the allocation of human resources is made for each school; teachers, administrators, secretaries, counselors, school nurses, food service people, custodians, etc.

F. The Evaluation Plan

This plan should outline clearly what instruments, techniques, and point of view are to be employed in evaluating the progress of children and professional staff members as they implement the instructional plan. The building must *not* get in the way of the instructional program.

G. The Support Plan

This plan describes the resources and services available to support the instructional plan. It should be developed by the chief school officer and have the blessings of the board of education. It is based on the requirements for personnel, materials, and school plant facilities to name just a few of the items which must be considered.

Chapter 3

The Design Phase

It is during this phase that staff members become involved in the writing of educational specifications. Also, the selection of the architect is made early in this phase.

As stated earlier, it is mandatory that everyone involved in the building program keep in mind that the building's only purpose is to house the educational program of that school. Regardless of how attractive a building may seem, unless it specifically meets the needs of that educational program, the building is inadequate.

The activities of the educational program must be considered as well as the course content. What are the pupils and the teachers actually going to be doing, both as groups and individuals? Traditional buildings have been designed around how teachers teach; thus, we have arrived at school design which permits the grouping of one teacher with twenty-five to thirty students for instruction. In this instructional mode, it has been the teacher's job to talk and the student's job to listen and remember what the teacher has said. Learning has been basically a passive activity in which remembering has had a higher priority than thinking. This has been, with minimum variations, the pattern of public education for several generations.

A more recent trend, however, is to design schools around concepts of how students learn, rather than simply how teachers teach. An additional modern concept is that students do not learn from a single source, but from many sources... including each other. If this concept is accepted, the teacher cannot be identified as the only source of instruction and information. The advent of the use of the computer in the classroom has changed forever the role of the teacher as being the only source of information in the classroom.

This has required that the focus shift from the teacher as the most important single factor in a school to the learner as the most important single factor in the school.

Present day construction should reflect this shift in emphasis from the teacher to the learner as the focal point of the school, as well as reflecting the changing role of the teacher. This allows the teacher to function as more than a lecturer, as more than a dispenser of knowledge. The teacher becomes increasingly a "motivator", one who will stimulate learning without readily giving the answers to students questions, one who will point the student in a direction which will permit students to discover answers for themselves.

In order for the teacher to adequately fulfill this role, it is necessary that a great number of educational tools be at his disposal, including the many audiovisual devices not included in instructional practice, as well as access to computer terminals and the assistance on non-certificated adults who will function in prescribed instructional roles.

In the design of an educational facility, the challenge in defining the educational program to be housed in the new school is not actually to pre-decide what form education is to take during the lifetime of that building, but rather to design an educational system which can retool itself to meet change as this change unfolds. Therefore, one key to good design is FLEXIBILITY — flexibility in space utilization, time utilization, and in grouping for instruction.

Of prime consideration is the number and kind of persons to be housed in the facility. Is it to be an elementary school with twelve classrooms expandable to twenty-four at some future date or expandable to large group instruction? Perhaps it could be a senior high school where the majority of the students drive their own cars to school. These types of considerations will certainly influence the size of the site as well as the design of the instructional area.

What are the space requirements for particular activities? It is generally accepted that different kinds of space are required for different kinds of activities, and that it takes more room and a different kind of space for a student in auto mechanics than it does for the student in American Government.

There are a number of publications which list space recommendations, including the Council of Educational Facility Planner's *Guide for Planning School Plants*, Michigan Department of Education's Bulletin #412 *School Plant Planning Handbook*, Utah State Board of Education's *School Plant Planning Series*, Colorado Department of Education's *Guide to Educational Planning for School Construction*, and several professional educational journals; AASA, ASBO, CEFP, as well as those by the American Institute of Architects (AIA).

Spatial relationships as well as space relationships must be considered. Certain educational activities should be placed in close physical proximity to each other, while others, because of their general characteristics, should be separated. For example, the Language Arts and Social Studies Departments should be located fairly close to the Library-Media Center. Industrial Arts and the Home Economics Departments can be located in the same area.

The band rehearsal room may be close to other noisy areas. However, the band should not be placed next to the English classrooms, nor should the Social Studies Department be placed next to the Metal Shop.

Increasingly in new schools there are requirements for special equipment in areas such as physical education, vocational, health, fine arts, science, language, business, and mathematics. The plans must provide for the use of this equipment, particularly if it involves the design of special conduit, ramps, or other such considerations.

Planning for the different media to be used in the instructional program should be considered in connection with special equipment. Of particular concern would be closed circuit television, adjustable lighting control for the use of audiovisuals, wiring for computer use, and provisions for acoustical control for both sound and vision recordings.

It should be remembered that all states now require that any building constructed with public funds be made accessible to and usable by handicapped persons. Provisions must be made for hand rails, ramps, signs, and other items required by law. Your architect will have access to the necessary requirements and documents which must be signed by the board of education to assure compliance.

It is vital that as many plans are developed, the community be informed of the ideas behind those plans. Most new schools appear to have features identified as "frills" by many members of the general public. Unless the public understands the thinking behind items such as carpet, air conditioning, swimming pools, exterior landscaping, and attractive interior decorations, it may feel that there is a gross waste of public funds. This is particularly true in communities in which other public buildings are not similarly equipped. Therefore, it is necessary that all of these so-called "frills" be explained to the community and that the community's feelings be tested as the educational specifications are written.

Don't skimp on the educational specifications. Educational specifications (ed specs) will be discussed in more detail later, but it should be pointed out at this stage that without educational specifications the architect builds his own building with little consideration for the educational programs which will be conducted in the building. The educational specifications for any new school should be written by the local teaching and administrative staff, but based upon educational goals established by the community.

It may be desirable to employ an outside consultant to guide in this activity, but teachers, administrators, and citizens know better than anyone else the educational needs of the local children and the kinds of tools which will be most effective in meeting those needs. However, their inability to articulate positive ways to reach those goals may result in their acceptance of lesser goals.

The educational specifications should be written for the optimum, most desirable, educational program. Go for the best educational program you can design and develop the building to fit that optimum educational program. You may have to cut back later, because of limited resources, but don't start designing a building to house a poor or mediocre educational program.

By designing for the optimum educational program, you will prevent the building from getting in the way of the teaching. The educational specifications should define program need as related to the physical characteristics of the building.

There should not be schematics or floor plans included in the educational specifications. The physical requirements should be described in detail in writing as well as the activities to be conducted within those programs, but the architect should be held responsible for translating these descriptions into a physical plant. Floor plans or other drawings submitted to the architect will limit the creativity of that architect.

The educational specifications should be based on the mid-life of the building and not on present acceptable levels of instruction or on current needs of teaching. Again, flexibility is one of the keys. A building designed in the 1980's should be expected to be in use well into the 21st century. It must not be obsolete within five to ten years of construction.

As the board and administration considers the development of the plan, they should check to make sure all of the following points are considered:

1. Adequacy of the new facility to house the desired educational program.
2. The aesthetic qualities of the building.
3. The compatible grouping of instructional areas.
4. The accessibility of the facilities to those who will be using them.

5. Adaptability and flexibility of the facility.
6. Community use.
7. Environmental controls including lighting, heating-cooling, and acoustical.
8. Safety.
9. Adaptation of the facility to the site.
10. Site development, size and location.
11. Ease of maintenance of the facility and grounds.
12. Relationship of facility to community planning, site development, and architectural compatibility with neighborhood and in keeping with community usage.

Selection of the Architect

As previously discussed, one of the most important steps the board will take is the selection of the *right* architect for the building program. A board should not limit itself to looking only at local architects. In the selection of a project architect several factors should be taken into consideration:

1. *Registration and professional reputation*
Only licensed architects only should be considered for any school construction. While this is required by most state's laws, some states still permit schools to contract directly with local contractors for school construction. This is a very bad practice for many reasons; insurance coverage, design reliability, supervision of construction, performance bonds, etc.

2. *Architect's staff and facilities*

The architect should have staff enough to complete all of the design phases of the planning on schedule.

3. *The architect's interest in the project*

Regardless of all other qualifications, only an architect who possesses a sincere interest in the design of the facility should be considered. The project should be one which the architect considers a challenge to his experience and ability and not another routine task for his company. Make certain that the architect interviewed will really be *involved* personally.

4. *The quality of work the architect has done in the past*

Though there are notable exceptions, the best indicator of future performance is the work which the architect has done in the past. The board of education should insist on firm standards of quality it expects from the architect. The board should demand that the architect design a building that meets the requirements of the educational program and is anesthetically pleasing. Boards have too often been satisfied simply with the use of low cost materials and a project designed to meet a low budget.

These objectives, however desirable, must be secondary to the adequacy in terms of housing the educational program. A competent, creative architect will incorporate these economic factors, and, if allowed, will provide an interesting and functional environment for the learning process. Remember, in the selection of the architect as in most things, you get pretty much what you pay for . . . and ***most districts are too poor to buy cheap.***

When considering an architect, some specific questions to be considered are:

1. Do contractors like to bid on the architect's plans?
2. How many change orders did boards experience in previous projects of the architect?
3. How well did the architect check availability of materials prior to bidding previous jobs?
4. Did he meet building deadlines"
5. Was there general satisfaction in closing out the project?
6. What kind of on-site supervisory services did the architect or his staff perform?
7. Did the architect work well with advisory committee and check their suggestions?
8. How willing is he to adhere to safety codes and other standards prescribed by law?

Suggested Steps in Architect Selection

1. Examine applications from several firms. Ask other sources for recommendations on applicants.
2. Narrow field to no more than three to five firms. Plan interview with each of these. Do *not* try to see more than one firm during a single interview session.
3. Visit a building or buildings designed by each of the architect candidates. Ask opinions of clients, contractors, and users of the structures. If time permits, use check sheets on evaluations. Most state education agencies have materials which can help in this evaluation.

4. Plan final interviews with one or two firms which would probably meet the district's needs. Before this session, ask chosen firm(s) to make a presentation based upon preliminary educational specifications. If necessary, be prepared to pay a nominal fee for this courtesy.

Six Basic Services the Architect Should Provide During the Planning Process

1. *Pre-Design Planning*

   The most important pre-design activity is the preparation of the educational specifications. While the professional staff will have basic responsibility for the development of these specifications, the architect should be connected closely with the development of these specifications. This will allow him to proceed step-by-step with the professional staff as the program requirements for the building are developed.

2. *Schematic Design*

   These are the initial drawings which translate the educational specifications into schematics for the physical plant. This is the first time floor plans as such will be introduced.

3. *Design Development*

   After the approval of the schematics, the architect will proceed to develop the basic design of the building. Plans will be studied and evaluated against the educational specifications. Elevations, models, and sketches will be developed by the architect to establish the physical characteristics of the project. Also, during this phase of the development, the architect will revise and make more detailed reports of the cost estimates of the building. He can also make preliminary recommendations regarding furniture and equipment.

4. *Construction Documents*

   After the design development has taken place, the architect will proceed with construction specifications and develop a set of working drawings. In broad terms, these establish quality, size, shapes, locations, relationships, as well as the standards for construction types of materials, manufacturers, and detailed drawings. The architect should submit his first revised cost estimates during this stage. He should also certify to the board that the plan(s) have been approved by the state education agency and other approving authorities.

5. *Bidding*

   The architect should assist the board in the development of bidding procedures, the advertising of bids, and the amount of contracts. Together, the board and administration will determine how the project is to be bid and from which contractors bids will be accepted. *It is important that the school attorney also be involved at this stage* to make certain all legal requirements are being met; legal notifications, time lines and dates which must be met, required legal documents, etc.

   The architect should be responsible for answering questions prospective bidding contractors will have regarding the project. With the school attorney, the architect should be held responsible for assisting the board in the awarding of contracts to the successful bidders.

6. *Construction*

The architect is the board's "man-on-the-job" in the supervision during the construction phase of the school. The architect should be responsible for determining schedules of payments, work progress schedules, and should make recommendations to the board regarding the possibility of "fast-tracking" the entire project. The architect should explain the "fast-tracking" concept to the board and administration. This procedure may save not only time but also considerable money.

The architect will issue bulletins and change orders as approved by the board and make frequent visits to the site to judge the progress and quality of the work, and that the work is progressing according to plan. Based on applications for payment by the contractors, he will recommend the board pay the contractor during the construction phase. He should be held responsible by the board for rejecting unacceptable standards of workmanship and will advise the board if this workmanship does not meet the standards established in the construction specifications.

As completion date of the project approaches, the architect will be responsible for collecting all required bonds, guarantees, and related construction documents from the contractor. He will develop a punch list for the use of the contractor. The items on the punch list should be corrected prior to the board's acceptance of the building.

Immediately upon selection of the project architect, a written contract should be drawn between the board of education and the architect. Oral agreements too often lead to future confusion and dissension. The contract should be definite, particularly in regard to rate and time payment to the architect and services to be performed by the architect prior to the bond issue election.

The fact the contract should be specific as to the service to be performed by the architectural firm cannot be overemphasized. Included in the services which may be performed are the preparation of the district's master plan for facilities; and preparation of preliminary drawings, working drawings, building specifications, and the necessary detailed drawings; the drafting of forms and proposals; the assisting and taking of bids; preparation of contracts; checking contractor's application for payment prior to the district's making payment to the contractor; the supervision of building addenda and change orders; and the general supervision and administration of the construction project. It is essential that whatever items above are agreed upon by the board and the architect be placed in the architect's contract.

The board of education may wish to hire its own "clerk of the works" who is responsible directly to the board. This individual would spend full-time at the construction site, which is not possible for the architect to do. This provides another check to insure quality control and proper construction. The "clerk of the works" should have a detailed understanding of construction, but need not be an architect or engineer. The author has made good use of retired contractors and retired superintendents of schools in this role.

Educational Specifications

As the educational specifications are developed, each group involved in their writing must assume certain responsibilities. According to the Council of Educational Facilities Planners, individual and group responsibilities for the writing of educational specifications might be defined as follows:

Board of Education

- Adopts permissive and guiding policies.
- Approves the official and written product.
- Authorizes the service of consultants.
- Employs specialists.
- Approves committees.

Administration

- Designates the director of the study committee and assists in the selection of the other members of the committee.
- Provides leadership, guidance, and assistance to the working committee throughout the study.
- Evaluates the progress.
- Interprets the results to the board of education, the staff, and the citizens of the community.

The Working Committee
(Teachers, students, administrators, citizens, etc.)

- Is responsible for the organization of the study.
- Accepts responsibility for the assignment and plans its activity.
- Identifies the needs, objectives, and goals of the school.
- Prepares a written report based upon the findings of the study.
- Reports to the administrator through its chairman.

Educational Consultant

- Provides guidance and response materials.
- Interprets discernible trends and new programs.
- Assists in the editing of the finished specification.
- Interprets the finished specifications to the design professions.

Architect

- Acts in the capacity of an observer and consultant during the program development.
- Serves as an advisor on architectural considerations.

An Outline for Educational Specifications

1. A brief statement of the school and community's goals.
   - Is this a community school meeting the need of all age groups, or a building designed to meet a unique need as determined by the district's educational philosophy?
2. A summary or a brief description of the major curriculum components.
   - Are the programs designed for non-college boundstudents as strong as those programs designed for the college bound?
   - What performance outcomes are to be expected from each of the curriculum components?
3. A description of the student and staff organization.
   - How many students will be housed in the facility as it is designed?
   - How many students might be accommodated by anticipated additions?
   - What provisions are made for large group and small group instruction and individual study?
4. A description of the typical student day.
   - Will the building be an "open" or "closed" campus?
   - Will the schedule be modular or conventional?
   - Will the structure of the classes be ungraded or conventional?
   - How much of the student's time will be spent in individual or computer-assisted learning?
5. A description of the typical teacher day.
   - Will there be work space for each staff member?

- Will each work space have access to a computer terminal?
- What is the anticipated student-teacher relationship?
- Will the learning environment be formal or informal?
- What teaching methodology will be most prevalent?
- To what extent will aides and other paraprofessionals be used?

6. A general description of the desired physical characteristics of the school.
   - What are the furniture and equipment needs?
   - Project time and space utilizations?
   - What provisions are made for thermal, visual, and acoustical control?
   - What kind of space flexibility is required?
   - What are the special considerations required including multi-media presentations, responsibilities to physically handicapped, unique maintenance problems, or special programs?

7. The detailed list of major space components.
   - What specific activities will be carried on in each major space?
   - What are the specific space requirements needed for those activities?
   - What are the site requirements for those particular activities?

8. A graphic representation of spatial relationships.
   - Are vocational and academic instruction areas properly integrated?

- Will the instructional materials center be centrally located, or placed in the traditional library?
- Are the noisy areas adequately isolated from the quiet areas?

9. A description of special functions and environmental considerations.
   - What special use will be made of lighting?
   - What special use will be made of accent color and texture?
   - What are the general and special safety factors to be considered?
   - Will the needs of physically handicapped and aged individuals be considered?

Avoid Planning Errors

The description of the educational specifications should prevent the making of many of the following kinds of planning errors:

1. Building a facility without really knowing and thinking through the needs that facility is to serve.
2. Prevents any of those involved in the building program from taking the attitude, "Let someone else do it."
3. Should cut down on improper use of information and research.
4. Failing to consider the latest trends and developments in good educational practice.

5. Not adequately organizing for planning.
6. Not involving a broad base of individuals and groups in the responsibility for planning.
7. Taking unilateral action without regard to scheduling activities.
8. Placing the educational program planning in the hands of an architect without giving him adequate information as to how he should relate the design of the building to the anticipated educational program or to the community to be served.
9. Not having an adequate document by which to evaluate the work of the architect.
10. Devoting too little time to adequate planning.

Again, it is *not* recommended that the professional staff include any kind of floor plan or schematics design with the educational specifications. Such a design would limit severely the professional creativity of the architect.

In dealing with secondary school facilities particularly, it is important that all current subject matter areas be considered. Included in the traditional scheme are such areas as English—including drama, speech, and journalism; mathematics; science; social studies; foreign languages; industrial arts and crafts; home economics; business and commercial subjects; art; music; physical education and health instruction; library services; as well as guidance services and facilities.

Many of these disciplines have adopted more of a laboratory approach rather than the 30X30 foot classroom where the teacher does all the talking to 20 to 30 students. In planning secondary schools provisions should be made for post high school and adult education classes unless some sort of vocational-technical center is immediately available to those community adults.

There should also be a statement regarding use of the library or the instructional materials center, as well as auditorium, cafeteria, kitchen facilities, guidance and counseling areas, the administration suite, health facilities, the adequacy of storage, as well as staff and student lounges and workrooms if they are to be provided.

Legal Advice and Fiscal Considerations

The arrangement for legal services at the beginning of any construction project is highly recommended. The attorney should be in a position to check the legality of every step of the program, particularly all negotiable instruments and contracts. This has particular significance in the bonding procedure.

In addition to this attorney, it is recommended that a bonding specialist or fiscal agent be employed to check all legal procedures followed by the district in acquiring permission to bond and in selling the bonds after a favorable election. Appropriate advice on investment of the proceeds from sale of the bonds is also needed.

Selection of a fiscal agent presents different problems than does selection of an architect. First, the attorney for the school district should play an integral part in fiscal considerations. Second, the board and its attorney should be aware of which bonding attorney the prospective fiscal agents intend to work through. Third, a check of the prospective agent's past performance with other school districts is basic. Only in this way can a district be aware of the fiscal efficiency of an agent or his company.

Site Selection and Development

School sites should be selected and acquired well in advance of the actual need. The selection of a site will involve technical problems as well as educational considerations which will require both educator and non-educator participation. Consideration should be given to the following factors in site selection:

1. Size and shape to meet the needs of the educational program.
2. Topography
3. Accessibility (to include traffic congestion, pedestrian traffic, bussing, or cycling)
4. Environment
5. Safety and health of pupils and school personnel
6. Accessibility of utilities and services, soil conditions, both surface and subsurface, the orientation of the building on the site, the initial cost and development cost, the relationship between this site and the location of other schools in the district, and most important of all, the location of the site with respect to the location of the students the school is designed to serve.

The size of the site will be determined by the nature and scope of the educational program of the school to be placed on that site. Site size is a local consideration, but the following would be recommended minimums:

Elementary Schools

It is suggested that the minimum *usable* size of an elementary school site be ten acres, plus one acre for each one hundred students to be housed in that school. Therefore, an elementary school of five hundred pupils would have a site of fifteen usable acres.

Junior High and Middle Schools

It is suggested that a minimum of twenty acres plus one acre for each one hundred students be provided for the junior high and middle school sites. Thus, a junior high of five hundred students should be located on a campus with a minimum of twenty-five usable acres.

Senior High and Combination Junior-Senior High

It is suggested that a minimum of thirty acres plus one acre for each one hundred students be provided for a senior high facility. Thus, a senior high school with an anticipated enrollment of one thousand students would be placed on a site of at least forty acres. The larger school site for secondary facilities is made necessary for a number of reasons: athletic fields, pupil and faculty parking, public use of the facilities, etc.

Where possible, it is strongly recommended that the schools cooperate with other municipal agencies in developing adjacent properties which could be used in combination with parks and school playgrounds. Consideration should also be given to the development of the site as outdoor and ecological laboratories.

Chapter 4

The Selling Phase

It is during this phase those who have been involved in the first three phases must convince the community at large of the need for additional or replacement facilities. Unless the general public is convinced the schools need more space, it is reluctant to vote funds for that purpose. In dealing with the selling of the idea of additional facilities, honesty is a basic necessity.

Don't cry "wolf." Far too many school administrators have declared a need for more space or more money, but when the buildings or funds are rejected, it is still "business as usual." The lack of funds, the cuts in programs were either unwisely anticipated or the programs were cut in such a way that the public was unaware there had been a program cut. If you are going to shout "emergency", you had *better* have an emergency.

Use of the following concepts may help a board or local administrator in selling an honest, needed proposal:

1. Remember that *the schools belong to the public.* Therefore, the public is entitled to know and participate in the planning of these facilities.
2. Release only complete and honest information to the public. Make certain that only those who are knowledgeable about the proposed project make public statements in the district's name.
3. Stress repeatedly that *the educational program is the only justification for the new school.* The educational needs, as identified in the educational specifications, should be made clear to the voting public.
4. Seek ways of broadening citizen involvement in the building project. Most people tend to support those activities in which they are asked *honestly* to participate.
5. Keep in mind some of the basic rules of communications; a large group is fine for dispensing information, but only in small groups or on an individual basis are attitudes or opinions actually changed.
6. Concentrate on those "publics" with whom you have some chance of success. Focus your resources where they will have the greatest effect; on those publics which are basically undecided. Point out, in the campaign, that the increased birth rate is not the only or possibly even the major cause for the need for additional space. Other factors would include:

    A. Costs for education have gone up. Public schools are the most expensive single item in the state or local governments.
    B. Schools are expected to do more than they have in the past, and are to do more for more people.

Virtually every social, economic, or political problem has been placed at the school-house doorstep during the past forty years.

C. New technology and programs are expensive. Many of the most expensive courses taught in our high schools today didn't exist when the student taking them entered first grade. Classes for remedial, handicapped, vocational, and computer-based education are more expensive than the traditional classes.

D. School systems are competing for dollars with other needed services which also need more tax dollars. Included are fire and police protection, public libraries and museums, decent systems of public transportation and highways, adequate housing, health care and care for the elderly, parks and recreation, and many other worthwhile and worthy organizations and agencies.

E. Public education is now responsible for a large number of children who would have been taught in the private or parochial schools of the past. The closing of these schools seem to be an increasing trend in many communities.

F. Federal funds are most often used for programs with high visibility, but have not yet had a significant impact in most districts, certainly not great enough to relieve the local tax "crunch" caused by state or federally mandated programs.

G. Schools are getting older. Many were built prior to World War II, while many other were built in the 1950's. These buildings are becoming "used up", and are no longer cost effective, neither in dollars nor in educational programs. Most were not designed to provide for the needs of a modern educational program. These older schools must either receive extensive and expensive remodeling or be replaced.

If the public perceives the request for new facilities as being "the administration's bond proposal" or the "board's building program," the project has little chance of success. Too many voters feel that about the only real voice they still have in government, at any level, is when they step into a voting booth to vote in a school election. Often they will use this opportunity to register a negative vote as an outlet for frustrations against big government, big schools, big industry, or to express their feeling of a loss of identity with the schools.

As stated earlier, possibly the most important single factor in an election campaign is the solid front presented by the board, the administration, the school district staff, and the citizens who have studied the problem thoroughly. If the need is not unanimously recognized by these groups, it is questionable that it will be recognized by the electorate.

On the other hand, if the board, administration, and the lay citizens involved use the same well-grounded facts, then the general public is more likely to perceive there is a need for new or remodeled facilities. A number of communications techniques should be used including open houses, displays in local businesses, tapes, films, clips on the local radio and television stations, the organization as speakers bureaus, and town council-type panel discussions.

Whether the campaign wins or loses, it is important that all of those who participated in the support of the proposal receive the sincere thanks and appreciation of the board and the administration.

Chapter 5

The Financing Phase

There are a number of ways of financing school construction, just as there are for financing any other form of construction. The best advice is for districts to hire a competent, outside financial consultant to assist with fiscal planning of the issue.

There are several alternative methods of financing the construction, including:

1. Pay-as-you-go

This is desirable where a district can afford to make a cash outlay for its new construction rather than going into long-term debt. This system may save the district between 50 and 200 percent of the cost of the project in unpaid interest, depending on the interest rates and the length of payment available at the time. District funds for construction under the pay-as-you-go plan can be combined with state, federal, or other funds.

Cutting costs for the project by reducing site costs should be considered. Site costs might be reduced by considering the use of public lands, particularly through the use of urban renewal credits. But don't put a multi-million dollar building on a poorly located site just to economize.

Another consideration for a pay-as-you-go plan is through the use of non-tax revenues. Sale of school-owned land or property is a method which might be also be used to raise money for construction. This step should be taken only on the advice of legal counsel.

2. Bond Issues

This is the most typical way in which districts raise construction funds. The most common form of bonding instruments in this case is the general obligation bond. The sale and use of bonds is strictly controlled by law. Because these bonds commit future boards and taxpayers, state laws require that these bonds be approved by the voters of the district.

To prevent districts from obligating themselves for more debt than they can logically repay, most state education agencies or state legislatures set definite limits on total bonding indebtedness.

3. Installment-Purchase and Lease-Purchase Agreements

This is a method which is being used frequently in the construction of school facilities. It is one which is used to finance smaller construction projects until more permanent solutions are found. Through this method the district finds an organization, private or public, which will finance and build the needed facilities. The leasing organization arranges its own method of financing, designing the building to meet the specifications established by the school district.

By using this method the school has no involvement as to how the money is raised. Installment purchases and lease purchase arrangements may be controlled by state statute, so the district should check the legal implications with the state department of education. An election is seldom necessary for these kinds of agreements. *Legal counsel should be sought before any installment-purchase or lease purchase agreements are signed between outside agents and school districts.*

Again, the best advice which may be offered a district regarding school construction financing is that it contact a recognized, competent bonding agency to work with the school attorney in the planning and sale of any bonds, whether they are serial bonds, straight term bonds, sinking fund-type bonds, or a combination of these.

Remember, a bond is a legal contract and courts have consistently held that every step taken in the authorization and sale of bonds is a part of that contract, including the election procedure, notice of sale, bid forms, authorizing procedures, and delivery of the bonds. The bond attorney should review each step of the process in concert with the local school attorney.

Chapter 6

The Construction Phase

It is during this period that a good architect, almost regardless of his price, with save a district money. It is critical that the architect be capable of personally supervising and inspecting the project while it is in progress. While a district-employed "clerk of the works" might be of value, only an architect is in a position to check adequately whether what is going into the building is what was designed.

The architect will play a vital role functioning between the owner, who is the board of education, and the contractor. In this role the architect should inspect and supervise construction within predetermined limits. The limits should have been determined in the contract written between the owner and the architect prior to the design-phase of construction.

As the representative of the owner, he will advise and consult with both the owner and the contractor during various phases of the construction. He will advise and consult with the owner in order to recommend changes in design which should be made regarding different materials which might be used. He will advise and consult the contractor in interpreting the owner's wishes and desires which are not specifically outlined in building specifications.

It should be made clear that the architect is not responsible for construction methods, techniques, schedule of construction activities, or safety. These items are the contractor's responsibility. However, the architect should visit the site frequently enough to assure the owner that all building specifications are being followed, and that the construction documents are all in place and available for examination.

The architect should advise payment to the contractor based on work completed. This advice should include both recommended payment schedules and the amount of payment.

The architect shall review the contractor's shop drawings as they are presented to him. He will assure the owner that the shop drawings are in compliance with the specifications designated in the general construction specifications document. The architect will also prepare change orders as they are required.

It should be pointed out that change orders are very expensive and should be avoided where possible. Adequate preplanned building specifications and educational specifications should prevent many major change orders during the construction phase, though a few will occur, even in the best planned construction.

On large projects, the architect may place a full-time representative of his office on the job. This person is most often not an architect, but is usually an experienced construction supervisor. He may have been a foreman or superintendent of construction projects or even the head of his own construction organization.

The purpose of this project representative is to assure than no corners are being cut in the actual construction operation and that quality materials are being used. This person might serve in much the same manner as the board's "clerk of the works".

The architect must assure the owner that all building codes are being met during the construction phase. It is the architect's responsibility to advise the owner when building codes are not being met, whether these are local, state, or federal building codes. It is also the architect's responsibility to then work with the contractor to remedy all building code violations and assure the owner that these violations have been corrected.

Chapter 7

The Occupation and Inservice Orientation Phase

M ost school buildings tend to be used during their entire lifetime much the same way they were used during the first few days of their occupancy. If a building is designed around an instructional program, all of the teachers and as many of the children as possible should be made aware of what that educational program is to be.

This should be done well in advance of their actual move into the facility. Otherwise, both students and teachers will simply transfer an obsolescent educational program into a new and modern facility.

The most common practice is still to move the furniture into the building the day after it is completed, and move the children and teachers into the building "cold turkey" soon thereafter, with the school operating full-bore by the second day of occupancy. This is a very poor way of introducing potentially innovative teachers and highly motivated students to the new facility.

In-service training for the teachers and administrative staff should begin during the writing of the educational specifications. It is during this period that the educational program is defined which is to be housed in the new school. If teachers are not involved in the writing of the educational specifications, chances are that they will continue to teach very much as they were teaching in the old facility.

Students moving into a new facility expect new and interesting educational processes. This enthusiasm is very short-lived, however, if they find the teachers and the educational program are basically the same as those they left in the old school.

The community, too, should be involved in the orientation phase. To some taxpayers, modern educational facilities seem to include a number of "frills". Included in the listing of "frills" might be items such as swimming pools, carpeted classrooms and halls, closed circuit television, computer terminals, and many other modern pieces of equipment and construction materials.

If the community understands the reasons for the inclusion of such equipment and building materials prior to the school's opening, the chances of acceptance of these new ideas are much better, though certainly not guaranteed . . . regardless of the prior orientation.

Chapter 8

The Evaluation Phase

Quite often this phase is overlooked entirely. Once the open-house is held, other professional educators and the local public tend to accept the building "as is" for the rest of its functional life.

There should be, for the sake of future planning, a detailed and careful analysis of all of the previously-mentioned phases as well as the functional design of the building. This evaluation should take place not later than the conclusion of the first year of occupancy. Otherwise, shortcomings are forgotten, good ideas for future construction are lost, and the same mistakes are repeated the next time around.

The form the evaluation is to take will depend on the desires and the needs of the local situation. The evaluation of the new school facility, however, should include at least these following points:

1. The general appearance of the building.
2. The appearance of the site and grounds.

3. General educational adequacy, including such items as the size and shape of the rooms, spatial relationships, student traffic patterns, instructional storage areas, etc.

4. Adequacy of support facilities, including cafeteria, administration and counseling offices, student lockers, toilets, drinking fountains, bus loading areas, custodial and maintenance workrooms, the ease of operation and maintenance, etc.

5. Adequacy of the learning environment and safety, including heating and cooling, lighting, ventilation, color and texture schemes, evacuation patterns, projections into halls or other student traffic patterns, slick floor areas, emergency lighting, etc.

6. Adequacy of the educational specifications; — did the educational specifications written by the staff and administration adequately provide and describe the hoped-for educational program and the program of student activities which would be housed in the new facility? What additions or corrections should be made in the writing of the next set of educational specifications?

There should also be brief evaluations of both the architect and the general contractor. The items to be evaluated should be shared with the architect and the contractor *prior* to the start of construction. They have the right to know how they are to be evaluated. The evaluation of the architect should include at least the following:

1. How well did the architect adhere to design, reporting, and construction schedules?
2. How adequate was the architect's staff for this project?
3. How adequate was the architect's on-site supervision and inspection?
4. What was the working relationship between the owner and architect and the architect and the contractor?
5. Did the architect forget the project once it was completed or did he show continued interest as to how well the building was working?
6. Was the architect's creativity and ingenuity adequate in translating the educational specifications into brick and glass?

The evaluation of the contractor should include:

1. Adequacy in providing quality experienced supervisors and workers.
2. Adequacy in meeting construction schedules.
3. Attitude toward correcting construction mistakes pointed out by governmental inspectors, the owners, or the architect.
4. Adequacy in control of subcontractors to assure quality workmanship.

Chapter 9

Do We Build New Facilities or Remodel?

We may call it remodeling, renovating, rejuvenating, or retrofitting, or something else, but it usually means about the same thing to most people; we're taking an old building and trying to make it new.

School buildings are expensive. *New* school buildings are even more expensive. As stated earlier in this book, one of the most difficult decisions any school district has to make is whether to get involved in a building program. It is expensive. It is time-consuming. It throws the school board on the mercy of the district's voting taxpayers. One of the most fearsome aspects of a building program is that, along each step of the process, the board makes decisions which are irreversible, once the process gets in motion.

Tommy Huckabee, of Huckabee Associates, AIA, states that, "The first hurdle for most school boards and citizens is to admit that their schools are, in fact, obsolete. The classrooms in these schools may be so familiar that they are accepted without receiving critical appraisal. They may be the very schools which board members themselves attended twenty years or more ago." Huckabee goes on to say that the older schools may have considerable aesthetic appeal and many are symbols of tradition and permanency in the community.

A more realistic view, however, might find that these schools are educationally and environmentally substandard. They are dark, have drab halls, are old and uncomfortable. The rooms are often too small, the chalkboards are old and unwriteable, the wood trim is dirty and hard to clean. Windows and doors are poor light sources and the lighting fixtures don't produce enough light or not the right kinds of light, with glare or bright/dark spots. The heating is inadequate and the ventilation is nonexistent. The toilets and urinals smell bad and the drinking fountains are inadequate and even unsafe.

All of these conditions happen a little at a time, with the board and community conditioned not to see the things which are happening to the school building over time. Age, by itself, should not be a factor in the evaluation of older school buildings. The physical condition of the building, its location in relationship to the student's homes, and the potential for remodeling are certainly more important.

It is difficult to develop an acceptable scale against which to measure the suitability of an old school building for its potential as a remodeling project. It is vital, however, that the school board, with the help of the administration and a licensed school architect, develop a criteria from which to determine whether to build a new building or attempt to remodel the old facility. Cost is certainly a factor, at this point.

The ideal educational facility should always be described, whether the new facility will be a new school or a renovated/remodeled building. The cost factor then comes into play as the board, administration, and superintendent measure the educational needs against the money available. The older building might be a candidate for remodeling . . . or it might not. It might be just too expensive to bring the old facility up to modern educational standards.

The reluctance to obligate large amounts of taxpayer money to school buildings has caused many school boards to consider three alternatives: 1) Build new school buildings, or 2) Remodel existing facilities, or 3) Put up some more "temporaries". There might also be a combination of the three, but most districts will select one of these three.

Building new schools will usually be the first choice of school boards: The facilities will look nice, will not require as much maintenance and up-keep, will permit the latest teaching methods and instructional aids (read especially "computers"), students and parents like the "new" building's looks, and the teachers will fight to see which of them gets to work in the new building. There is no question but what a new school building is the way to go . . . if the district can afford it or if the old buildings are not structurally sound.

The temporary, "modulars", have several features unique to the movable-classroom concept. First, they *are* less expensive. The cost of the modular is a fraction of what either new construction or remodeling would cost. Second, they may be placed on existing school grounds, with utilities extended from existing buildings. Parking space, playground areas, and support services (library, audio visual equipment, secretarial help, faculty lounge, health and nursing services, etc.) are already "on site". And modulars are cheap. These, and other reasons encourage school boards to select portable school buildings, rather than build or remodel.

But the modulars have many drawbacks, also. They are not very durable, often not lasting until they are paid for. Maintenance costs are very high. They are not constructed in such a way as to endure. They are usually not very attractive and neither students nor teachers will prefer to work in them. There are exceptions, but generally both teachers and students feel that they have left the school campus when they go "out back" to the modulars.

Often the school's intercom system is not wired into the portable so teachers and students in those buildings don't get announcements, the plumbing is all in "the main building", students and teachers get wet every time they must go the the gym or library or computer room or. . . . Seldom are there sufficient covered walkways between the modulars and the main building, so students, teachers, equipment and visitors are exposed to the elements when the weather turns bad.

There are many reasons both for and against portable buildings as classroom space.

So that leaves the school board with the consideration of renovating/remodeling/retrofitting an existing building.

If the basic structure of the existing school is sound, and only a structural engineer or architect can really tell, there is no reason why remodeling should not be a real consideration for the school district. Remodeling is less expensive than the construction of a new building. It is more expensive than buying modular classrooms, but the remodeled building will last for many more years and is a great deal more functional as classroom space.

A good architect can take the shell of an old building, if it is structurally sound and meets other criteria (location, parking space, expandability, etc.) "gut" it, and convert it into a building which is both attractive and educationally functional. The school district will want to select an architect which has a "track record" in school remodeling.

Cost is always a factor. The facility, whether new, remodeled, or modular, should live beyond its payments. While cost is a factor, *the vast majority of school districts are too poor to buy cheap.* It is a false economy to purchase facilities which are of poor quality, which soon require excessive maintenance, which become educational unsound or are soon unsafe for student and teacher occupancy.

For example: If you have an old school building which would cost $15,000,000 to replace, would it be more cost-effective to remodel the school for a cost of $5,000,000? The decision should be based on two factors; first, will the building be educationally sound for both present and future instruction, and, second, how long will the building be educationally and physically sound?

If a $15,000,000 school building can be remodeled for $5,000,000, extending the useful lifetime of the building 12-15 years, the remodeling funds might be well spent. If, however, for those 12-15 years the remodeling funds only put on an occasional new coat of paint onto an educationally inadequate building or changes a few interior walls, the savings will reflect a false economy.

Any remodeling must bring the facility up to a quality which would encourage a sound educational program. For example, many schools may be brought up to standards in safety, appearance, and space, but be totally unprepared to provide the wiring necessary for extensive multi-media and computer use. Such a facility would need to be replaced or remodeled again in the near future . . . and rewiring a school is expensive.

Some architects suggest a number of questions any school district should be able to answer before deciding whether to remodel an old building or build new facilities:

1. Should we remodel or build new? This is the basic question.
2. How do we decide?
3. What factors determine which way to go?
4. What does *this* school district mean by the term, "Remodel"?
5. Will remodeling save money? Will it save time?
6. Is it a good investment, remodeling an old building.
7. Will the remodeled facility serve the future educational program for 15-20 years?
8. Will the district be remodeling the old building into a new teaching-learning environment or will it simply be giving the old building a "face lift", trying to make it look like a *new* 1930's building?
9. Is the remodeling idea to save a building of historical significance or just nostalgia?
10. How does the cost of remodeling compare with the cost of a new building?
11. What is the age and structural/mechanical condition of the building being considered for remodeling?

12. Was the building constructed as one unit, originally, or have there been a series of "add-on" over the years.

13. How does the community feel about remodeling an old school? Would this help or hinder a bond proposal?

14. Will the building reflect community pride or a "gutless" school board and administration, applying "band aids" to the educational facilities problem?

Again, remodeling can mean a great many things to different members of the school district. In order to consider it as a possible alternative to the construction of new buildings or going "modular", everyone involved should be working from the same perspective.

The facility being considered for remodeling must first be structurally sound, but older schools are usually educationally obsolete. Most old buildings will need new plumbing and electrical wiring, but these costs are minor compared to the overall costs of a new building. The unlearned eye can't really tell whether that crack in the foundation is "cosmetic", not really that important, or "structural", which might cause the building to settle or even fall. Again, only a professional, an architect or structural engineer, can really advise you on that.

The proposed remodeling must provide for up-to-date teaching methods and equipment. Care must be taken to assure that a modern educational program may be provided in the remodeled building. It is not economical, neither in money nor educational practice, to attempt to clothe an inadequate facility with a modern educational design. It has long been said, in building circles, "form fits function", and in no place is that more true than in school remodeling.

As stated earlier in this book, the school building is only the envelope into which you slip an educational program. *It is not an end in and of itself.*

The majority of old school buildings are not on sites large enough to accommodate modern educational practices. The remodeling of the old school will not make the playground any larger or move the streets back away from the building or provide more parking for faculty, students, and visitors.

Most state departments of education will provide school boards with recommended, or in some cases required, minimum school site sizes. In many cases, it is possible for the school board to work with city and/or county officials to get an adjacent street closed in order to get more space for the school.

Many older schools are also located in older neighborhoods . . . which means that the people living around the school grounds are usually older people. There may be no more school-aged children in that neighborhood anymore. The school may now be in the wrong place, even though the building is structurally sound and would be suitable for remodeling. Kids grow up and leave, but in many cases the parents stay in the same community, just getting older.

The community may no longer provide young children who would be the students of the school. Communities, like their schools, get older. As they do, the schools are no longer needed to house and educate the young of that community.

School boards must be certain, before they commit to remodeling, that the building can be truly remodeled, not just undergo a "facelift". Some old schools may be made attractive from the outside, but still remain inadequate educationally. If the remodeling is only cosmetic, the educational program will suffer, particularly since teachers, students, parents, and taxpayers will expect a modern, state-of-the-art educational program to be placed in the renovated facility.

Frequently, it is hard for the older school to meet modern building and life safety codes. This is certainly a consideration before a school board elects to remodel an old school. It may cost too much to bring the building up to code. It may be more expensive than the remodeled facility would be worth.

The faculty and administration should be consulted concerning the "teachability"of the building, as well as whether the school may be properly administered. The administrative questions center around four points:

1. Safety
2. Site
3. Space organization and adequacy
4. Maintenance

The concern for safety is of primary concern, being a higher priority that even the curriculum and instruction. Some old buildings are unsafe . . . period. Because of their basic design, they are unsafe for children and adults. Factors which might be considered, so far as *safety* are concerned, might include:

1. May the school busses load and unload out of the flow of traffic?

2. Do the student pedestrian traffic crosswalks and lights adequately control student traffic?
3. Are the playgrounds fenced where they border streets, ravines, or other hazards?
4. Are there ramps and other considerations for the handicapped?
5. Are the odds for slipping minimized on walks, stair treads, floors in food service areas and showers and toilets?
6. Is the lighting adequate, especially in halls, exits, stairwells, and backstage areas?
7. Is the building regularly inspected by a fire marshal?

Administrative considerations regarding the *site* might include:

1. Is the size of the site adequate? Does it meet state recommendations for this type school?
2. Are there drainage or erosion problems? These will show up first in the playground areas, particularly under the swings.
3. Is the site located near parks, student residences, playgrounds, swimming pools, or other recreational areas?
4. What is the neighborhood environment? Old slum-type housing, industry, sex shops, highways or railroads, etc?

Administratively, the study should also check the adequacy of the *space* to be used by the school:

1. Is there room for future expansion?
2. Is there a good plan for adequate student traffic flow in the halls and other passing areas?
3. Does the building provide enough space, and the right kinds of space, for staff requirements; storage, dining, conferencing, and planning?
4. Are the classrooms, laboratories, lecture rooms, and library of adequate size and correctly located for maximum utilization?
5. Are the interior, non-bearing walls located and constructed so that they may be moved to fit future needs?
6. Are the ceilings too high for good lighting, ventilation, acoustics, etc?

The *maintenance* considerations, so far as the administrators are concerned, might include:

1. Does the exterior finish of the building require little or no maintenance?
2. Are the interior walls and floors of the classrooms and toilet rooms constructed with materials which require little or no repainting or maintenance?
3. Are the plumbing and utility lines properly located and protected from rust and corrosion?
4. Is the roof in good repair? Does it meet present standards and codes?
5. Have wooden sashes been replaced with aluminum, puttyless windows which require a minimum of maintenance?
6. Is there a maintenance plan for the building?

The faculty should be asked a different set of questions, regarding the needs for building replacement/remodeling. These questions center around four primary headings, though the list may certainly be expanded:

1. Acoustics
2. Lighting and electrical systems
3. Heating and ventilation
4. Equipment and furnishings

It is, for all practical purposes, impossible to teach in a classroom which has poor acoustics. This author, early in his teaching career, taught in a classroom where instruction stopped each time a desk was moved. It took seconds for the sound to stop bouncing around the walls, floor, and ceiling. If a student coughed, it took even longer to be able to hear.

That was the way schools were made, back when, and many of them are still in service . . . unimproved . . . today. When teacher or students weren't sliding desks or coughing, Mr. Jones, the school custodian, was watering the grass outside my classroom window . . . splat, Splat, SPLAT, **SPLAT** as the sprinkler moved across the windows. Again, instruction ground to a halt.

The classroom teachers should be asked a series of questions dealing with *acoustics*, whether the board of education is considering new construction or remodeling an existing facility:

1. Is it difficult for your students to hear and understand when you speak in a normal voice?
2. What might be done to reduce outside noise from the halls, traffic areas, playgrounds, etc?

3. Can you hear the class in the next room? Across the hall? Above your room?
4. Where does the most noise presently come from, assuming the noise sources should be eliminated with the planned new construction and/or remodeling?

   a. Heating and ventilating equipment
   b. Plumbing lines and fixtures
   c. Fluorescent lighting
   d. Floor waxers and buffers
   e. Outside disturbances
   f. Other classes in the building
   g. Other_____

Teachers should also be asked about *lighting and other electrical systems.* Natural lighting is fine, but can create glare spots and shadows which are hard on student's eyes. There may be dark corners and parts of the room where the student's hand creates a shadow on the paper on which he is writing or on the chalkboard which the teacher is using. Questions which might be asked of the teaching staff could include:

1. What kind(s) of lighting do you prefer? (Incandescent, concentric rings, indirect fluorescent, luminous ceilings, etc.)
2. Are the walls and ceiling surfaces dark or are they light, reflecting and diffusing the available light?
3. Is direct sunlight creating glare and eyestrain?
4. Are there enough electrical outlets of the proper size and voltage?

5. Is there proper night lighting in the halls, entrances, parking areas, and other places where teachers might be traveling at night?

Many years ago, teachers and students were granted two rights by those who determine such things. One is the right to be dry and the other is the right to be warm. Today, we have added a third; the right to be cool. *Heating and ventilation* play a big part in the education of a child.

Children can't properly learn, nor can teachers properly teach, if they are wet, or too cold, or too hot. The days of discomfort as a part of the educational process have passed. Kids know they learn best when they are comfortable. Teachers know this. Administrators know this. Parents know this. School board members know this.

While all these groups recognize the need for a "comfort zone", regarding heating and cooling, only the teacher is constantly aware of the effect of the thermal environment on the educational attitude of his/her students. Therefore, teachers should be asked questions concerning what they would like in the way of heating and cooling:

1. Is the temperature adjustable?
2. Does it vary from one part of the room to another?
3. Are there drafts?
4. Does the heating or cooling create an odor?
5. What do you do for ventilation when there are no windows?

Another part of the potential for remodeling criteria which may best be answered by the classroom teacher is that dealing with *equipment and furnishings*. The teacher might be asked:

1. Is the storage in your room adequate?
2. Are the chalkboards, map rails, pegboards in the right spots?
3. Do you have adequate display space?
4. Are the electrical outlets placed properly for A-V or computer equipment?
5. Is there enough counter space? (Recognizing that there *never* is enough counter space . . . or storage space . . . or bulletin board space!)
6. Was the classroom equipment selected for mobility, resistance to breakage, encouraging correct posture, and attractiveness?
7. Was the room "color coordinated"?

While the administration and faculty can and should be involved in the questions concerning remodeling or building from "scratch", it will be the responsibility of the board of education to make the ultimate decision: Do we build a new building? Do we remodel an old building? Do we put in some more modulars? . . . or do we just forget the whole thing and hope the next board will handle the problem?

With the move away from unique and award-winning radical school designs, particularly during times of low funding levels at both state and local levels, the remodeling/renovating/retrofitting approach is appealing to more and more school boards. There is no question but what new schools are nice, but they are also expensive.

With proper assistance from a good architect, with direction from the school administration, and with input from a concerned faculty, the school board should be in a position to make the tough decisions. These are hard decisions, made in hard times, but they will only get worst by postponement.

Summary

Again, it should be emphasized that a school building only houses an educational program. It must not become an end in itself. While the cost of the building involves only a very small part of the total educational cost of the things that will be going on inside its wall, lack of planning can cause the building to inhibit and severely restrict the educational program.

According to Dr. Harold Gores, former president of the Educational Facilities Laboratory, *over the lifetime of the school its cost represents only about **six percent** of the total amount of money spent on and in that building.* He states, "To put it another way, when you add *two* teachers to the school staff, their salaries and benefits for twenty years will equal the cost of a million-dollar building.

Yet school officials may discuss for five minutes the consequences of adding two teachers and then argue into the dawn the expenditure for a building. In short, *building costs are practically nothing when compared to the total educational scheme of things.*"

Educational specifications will play a major part in the development of an adequate school plant. The quality of these specifications is usually in director proportion to the time, resources, and educational leadership committed to their writing. These educational specifications should be written in clear, meaningful terms which are understood by professional educators, boards of education, lay citizen groups, and the general public. They should be in detail enough that the person reading them can visualize the educational program and activities which are to be housed in the new facility.

Those who are considering new facilities should review the files in the office of the state education agency. Current school construction within the state may be reviewed within a few hours in that office. This can save a district a great deal of time and money in determining architects for consideration, current building costs, as well as styles of construction being built within the state.

A board or administrator should not be reluctant to seek outside consultant assistance in the areas where they either feel inadequate to offer expert technical assistance, or in areas in which they simply do not have the time to devote to the technicalities and details of planning. Few districts have a continuing building program which would require keeping these kinds of people hired full-time. It is usually a great deal more cost-effective to contract with outsiders for those services.

There is no single guide which will totally cover all aspects in the planning of educational facilities. Each individual, unique school construction project presents its own problems. It is hoped, however, that this guide will assist members of boards of education, superintendents, and others concerned with the planning and building of school facilities to develop the best possible building in which to house the best possible educational program.

Appendix A

A Sample Facilities Study Project
(initial letter from consultant to superintendent)

Mr. Joe Texan
Superintendent of Schools
Textown Independent School District
P.O. Box 291
Textown, TX 76543   February 6, 1995

Dear Mr. Texan:

Thank you for inviting me to your school district yesterday. I appreciated the warm reception, and particularly appreciated the opportunity to observe (and almost get involved in) your National Honor Society initiation. Three of my children were members of that organization, so the ceremony brought back memories of my own kids "carrying the candles".

I would be happy to work with you and your district in making an evaluation of your existing facilities. I would propose an examination of the buildings in light of generally-accepted standards. I like to use those developed by the National Study of Secondary School Evaluation as well as those of the Educational Facilities Laboratory. These would give both comprehensive coverage and a standard of quality which is used nation-wide.

The study, as I envision it, should not take more than 20-25 hours of consulting time. During that time I would meet with the staff and administration discussing the educational needs of the buildings, make my own observations and comments regarding the facilities, develop both "straight-line" and survival enrollment projections, make some slides, and prepare a written report to present to the Textown Board of Education not later than April 30.

The consulting fee would be $100 per hour, plus $.28 per mile from my office in Granbury. There is certainly no charge for the initial meeting, which we held yesterday, or for travel time. The only time the "clock is running", so far as the fee is concerned, is when I could be actually working on your project.

I will keep a log of time spent which would permit your monitoring of the expenses as the project developed. A copy of my time-sheet would be submitted to you after each visit or after the follow-up office work-session, whichever you prefer.

If this is satisfactory with you and your Board of Education, please let me know and I will begin work within the next week. A contract, stating the above conditions, may be signed by both your board and Holcomb Associates at any time you might consider appropriate.

I will look forward to working with you, if you would like. If not, I still appreciated the opportunity to visit with you and meet members of your faculty and staff. Thanks for your hospitality.

Sincerely,

John H. Holcomb, CEO
Holcomb Associates
151 Tahiti Drive, The Shores
Granbury, Texas 76048
(817) 573-6203

Notes on Textown Consulting Job
(For Planner's Use Only)

Requested present room utilization plan, including schedules
and class sizes for each room. (Receive by February 10)
Establish time lines and PERT:
First meeting, February 5, with superintendent, elementary
principal, secondary principal.
Make bid for project, February 14.
Board report, April 30
Set dates to meet with staff, board.
Development of educational specifications?
Has own architect?
Superintendent mentioned 2 elementary schools, 24 classrooms
each, plus all-purpose library and other support services.
Board is in general agreement, though hate to commit at this
point. Also, both board and superintendent are starting to
discuss the need for a middle school/junior high.
Currently spending about $4,800 per pupil.
"Lake people", and other "people across the lake" are
considerations. Be interesting to see make-up of the board.
Look for better utilization of present facilities. A good
architect might salvage a couple of the elementary schools
and made them usable and educationally sound for the
next 15-20 years.
Get "site-development" rating sheet. (Created by March 15)
Elementary principal's offices should be looked at. Not usable
part of the day.
Projections are influenced by "pig-in-a-python"
considerations which will influence averages.
We get accustomed to seeing what we see without looking at
it. Board should be reminded of that.

Initial Presentation by Consultant to Superintendent and School Board

To Mr. Texan and Board of Education:

Introductory Comments and Guiding Principles:

The only justification for a school building is to house an instructional program. The costs of the buildings are only a very small percentage of the total cost of education which the buildings house. For example, you might spend $500,000 for a building to house 10 classrooms.

You should remember that, if you consider an average annual salary for 10 teachers at $25,000 each , the District would be paying $250,000 per year for that building in teacher salaries alone. If the building is to last for 30 years, at today's dollar rate, the District would be investing roughly $7,500,000 just in teachers salaries during the lifetime of the building for those 10 teachers.

This educational cost, just in teacher salaries alone, puts the cost of the school building itself into proper perspective.

Not providing those teachers and their students with an effective and efficient learning environment, in order to save a few dollars initially, isn't good business management.

The building may be a thing of beauty, but if it does not encourage good learning, it is not worth the cost. Most good learning facilities are attractive and encourage learning. Every study done indicates that students learn better when they are in pleasant surroundings.

The school plant, consisting of the site, buildings, equipment, and services, is a major factor in the functioning of the educational program. The plant, as planned and equipped, is more than a place of instruction. It is, during school time, the physical environment which assists or limits student achievement of desirable learning outcomes.

The school plant must provide the physical facilities to conduct a program designed to meet the educational needs of youth. This necessitates provisions for a variety of classroom, extraclass, recreational, and community activities. The plant must provide illumination, water, heat and ventilation, and sanitation services which contribute to the health of its occupants. The plant must also be designed, equipped, inspected, and maintained so as to minimize the possibility of accidents and fires involving its occupants.

The facilities, so far as possible, should be designed to accommodate future enrollment and program needs as well as present needs. Flexibility of use should be a feature of the buildings. The best combination of efficiency and economy should be sought.

Dr. John H. Holcomb, CEO
Holcomb Associates

Textown Site Evaluation Sheet

Site location: _____ Date of Inspection: _____
Persons Conducting Inspection: _____

General Description of Site:
    Shape:
    Size:
    Comments:

	Rating (1-low,5-high)
Topography:	_____
Drainage:	_____
Accessibility:	
General Traffic	_____
Parking	_____
Bicycles	_____
Pedestrian	_____
General Environment:	
Appearance	_____
Surrounding area	_____
Zoning	_____
Existing Utilities to Site:	_____
Existing Roads, Highways, Curbs and Gutters	_____

Soil Conditions, both surface and
    subsurface   _____

Orientation of building on site
    (utility)   _____

Location of other major buildings
    to site: (Stores, offices, commercial
    shops, etc)   _____

Location of homes of students in
    relation to site   _____

Comments:

Appendix B

Evaluation Instruments

Elementary Classrooms: (General)

1. Does the building design lend itself to a good elementary
    education environment? (General Comments)

2. Describe the appropriateness of the following specific
    areas of the school plant, including:
    a. Design of building: (Does the physical arrangement
        of the building get in the way of a good educational
        program?)

    b. Furnishings:

    c. Equipment:

d. Space for different activities: (Reading groups, individual study, etc.)

e. Teacher space, including tutorials:

f. Interest centers, work tables, small groups:

g. Audio-visual capability:

h. Access to multi-purpose room or assembly area:

i. Faculty room:

j. Access to library:

k. Classroom storage space:

l. Supply storage space:

m. Student restrooms:

n. Drinking fountains:

o. Art room

p. Music room

q. Computer room (If not present, but needed, what would be required?)

r. Health and sick room

s. Safety hazards noted

t. Provisions for handicapped

Additional comments:

Secondary Classrooms: (General)

1. Adequate room in the classroom to provide a minimum square footage per pupil. This should allow room for a teacher's desk, filing cabinet, lectern and chair. (Use architect's tables for standardized figures.)

2. **Each classroom** should have the following equipment:
   a. Chalkboard
   b. Overhead projector and screen
   c. Bookcases
   d. Storage space (probably the most overlooked need)
   e. Tackboard
   f. Display facilities
   g. Ability to darken room for audio-visual use
   h. Magazine display and storage facilities
   i. Student desks; movable for variety of activities.

3. **Special needs:**

   a. **Art room** needs sink with sediment traps, extra moving-around room, storage space, work space (for drawing, painting, modeling, carving, weaving, and printing), workbenches, electrical and gas outlets, wall surface treated for display, display racks or trays.
   Comments:

b. **Business Education room** needs acoustical treatment (so as not to interfere with other classes), typewriters and other business machines, storage for student work, storage for instructional materials and supplies, adjustable typing desks, typing chairs, filing equipment.
Comments:

c. **English rooms** need lots of book storage space, additional magazine and periodical racks, television sets with VCR's, access to transparency-producing equipment, audio recording equipment.
Comments:

d. **Foreign Language room** needs are basically the same as those for the English rooms, with the possible exception of a language laboratory, if enough foreign language is taught to warrant one.
Comments:

e. **Health and Physical Education rooms** need, in addition to the gym space, room for health education classes (equipped much like English classroom), tables for conducting experiments and demonstrations, library and reference materials, display and storage space, A-V capability. These facilities should be designed in such a way that they could be used by the community without opening the rest of the school, with restrooms which could be used by the public. Special attention should be paid to sanitation; drinking fountains, rest rooms, showers, dressing areas, etc. The architect would have national standards which should be met, as well as state and county standards which *must* be met.

Comments:

f. **Home Economics rooms** need plenty of hot and cold running water, portable screens, extra ventilation, small-group discussion areas, a "living center", equipment for cooking and meal service, first aid education equipment, space and equipment for child development, extra sink and disposal capabilities, adequate outlets for gas and electricity, modern home equipment.

Comments:

g. **Industrial Arts room** need outside entrances for off-loading materials and supplies, floors with special non-slip finishes, extra ventilation, access to water-gas-electricity, extra high ceilings, fire-resistant cabinets, easily cleaned floors and walls,

washing facilities, tool display boards and/or racks, lockable storage areas for supplies, finishing area, shop library, audio-visual capability.
Comments:

h. **Mathematics rooms** need graph or cross-section chalkboard, chalkboard instruments, models for prisms, pyramids, cones, etc.
Comments:

i. **Music rooms** need special acoustical treatment, high ceilings, located away from other instructional areas, storage for musical instruments, adequate piano space, room for risers, audio equipment, recording equipment, storage for robes and uniforms.
Comments:

j. **Science rooms** needs are much the same as those of the Industrial Arts rooms, so far as ventilation, heating, lighting, added water and gas, and demonstration and experimentation tables. Other similarities would include the access to first aid equipment and treatment, fans and hoods to remove obnoxious and toxic gases, secure tool and chemical storage facilities, different types of voltage outlets, and safe and secure storage for hazardous materials. An emergency shower should be provided in case of acid spills, etc. Comments:

k. **Social Studies rooms** should be designed somewhat the same as the English rooms, although additional wall space would be needed for graphs, maps, and other visuals. Extensive use of audio-visual materials by social studies teachers require that the rooms be darkened frequently. Comments:

l. **Library and Instructional Materials Center (whether used by elementary or secondary schools)** should be centrally located in order that all students and faculty will be able to make use of the service. It should have easy loading and delivery access, should be large enough to provide for good reading and study conditions (again, the architect has standards), should have good thermal-acoustical-lighting control, should be attractive and cause students to want to come to the library, should provide the librarian adequate work/office space, vertical files, A-V reproduction capabilities, and storage space for materials used by many teachers or which are seldom used.

Furnishings and fixed equipment for the library/IMC would include:

Adjustable shelving

Magazine shelving

Newspaper shelving

Tables and chairs of different size and height
(K-12 use)

Desks and chairs for staff

Charging desk

Dictionary stand

Atlas stand

Card catalog cases

Vertical file cabinets

Bulletin boards and a display area

VCR's and tapes

Display cases

One or more "trucks" for instructional materials and
equipment

Typewriter

Stools

Locker

Sink with hot and cold running water

"Stacks" areas, with cabinets, cases, shelving, or racks
for storage of materials, such as recordings, large
posters, maps, prints, films, filmstrips, slides,
tapes, etc.

Comments:

m. **Health Service room** should be more than a place for sick kids to go until their parents pick them up or it's time to catch the bus. It should be a place where a school nurse could provide counseling in a private environment, give examinations, render first aid, keep school health records, telephone parents and medical authorities, and confer with faculty and staff regarding student medical needs. This would require desk, chair, visitor(s) chair, file cabinet, telephone, cot, medicine cabinet with lock, toilet and washbasin, and a lockable door. It should be located near, but not in, the administrative offices.

Comments:

n. **Administrative Offices:** The central offices and related areas serve a specific role in education. It is a supportive one, necessary to permit the educational program to function. These spaces need to be specifically designed to fit the activities which are to be carried on in those spaces, to accommodate the essential items of furniture, equipment and supplies, and to provide comfortable, efficient working conditions. "Form to function" is at no point more required than in the administrative offices. The unique needs of Textown will be reflected in the design of the administrative area.

Each of the administrative offices should be capable of the following activities:

1. Receiving students, school personnel, and visitors to the school.
2. Studying, conferring, dictating correspondence and memoranda, and accounting by administrative personnel.
3. Typing, bookkeeping, record-keeping (by clerical staff), particularly in the central office.
4. Preparing and storing records.
5. Admitting new students, checking attendance and readmitting returning students.
6. Conferring with groups of parents, teachers, and/ or students, in privacy.
7. Conducting certain types of examinations, both physical and educational.
8. Central storage area (secure) for equipment and supplies.
9. Management of student and school activities.
10. Systems which provide effective communications within the building and with persons outside the building.
11. Provide work space for duplication machines, audio-visual materials, other work areas.

(1) **Superintendent's office:** The superintendent's office is the key communications point in the school district, if not in the community. All school activity eventually funnels through this office, whether it involves curriculum, personnel,

discipline, community activities, record keeping, federal and state reports, minutes of board meetings, transportation, food services, health services, community gripes or complements, messages for employees or students, handling correspondence, conferring with other superintendents, or the selection of gym seal. It should be light and airy, reflecting the image the board of education and community would like to leave on visitors regarding the type of district they are visiting. The school district is not only an educational institution, but it is also the biggest business in most communities. The business end of the school district, the superintendent's office, should reflect that concept.

The superintendent needs a conference room large enough to accommodate himself/herself and the members of the board of education with privacy. This room will be used for many purposes; district-level planning, curriculum study groups, parent group meetings, community groups, etc.

Comments:

(2) **Principal's Office:** The principal's' office should be located near the main entrance of the building. They should contain a small wardrobe storage closet. An outside entrance into the main hall is

desired as well as into the general office. The secretary's office should be large enough to accommodate a desk, chair, work table, typewriter and/or computer stand, telephone, and two waiting chairs. A counter to be used in dealing with student traffic is desirable. The principal's offices should be large enough to accommodate chairs for five or six persons in conference, an administrator's desk and chair, a medium-sized table, a bookcase, and two file cabinets. There should also be a typewriter/computer and table for the principal's use.

Comments:

(3) Faculty Lounge: This room should be planned for combined use by men and women. Lavatory facilities should be a part of this room or in the same area of the building. The lavatory doors should not open directly into the lounge. The room should be furnished informally and should contain two or three chairs, a divan, end tables, small book shelf and magazine area. Electrical outlets for lamps and other appliances are necessary. Space for a small cabinet with small sink, electrical outlet, hot plate or microwave, counter space, and storage shelving are strongly suggested.

Comments:

Individual Textown Teacher Opinionaire
Elem__Sec__Other__

(For evaluation of existing facilities.
Completed by the faculty and staff)

The following should be answered in the two columns on the right. The column marked (A) is "What should be?". The column marked (B) is "How well are we doing it?"

In "A", mark from 1 to 5, with 1 being "Should **not** be doing it", and 5 being "Should be doing it well." Marks of 2, 3 or 4 are in between.

In "B", mark from 1 to 5, with 1 being "We aren't doing it at all", and 5 being "We do it very well". Marks of 2, 3, or 4 are in between.

	"A"	"B"
1. The building allows the implementation of a program which complies with the philosophy and objectives of the Textown school district._____	____	____
2. The building encourages student learning and growth.	____	____
3. The school provides for space for special groups.	____	____
4. Heat and ventilation are well controlled.	____	____
5. Both artificial and natural lighting are well controlled.	____	____

6. Noise levels are appropriate for activities. ____ ____
7. Provisions are made for the health and safety of all personnel using the school building. ____ ____
8. Building permits free movement from one activity to another. ____ ____
9. Building makes good use of staff time. ____ ____
10. Building is flexible enough to make changes in enrollment or program. ____ ____
11. Equipment and facilities are appropriate in size and type for elementary student. ____ ____
12. The best possible use is being made of the building. ____ ____
13. The building is easily maintained and cleaned. ____ ____
14. There is adequate staff and visitor parking. ____ ____
15. The building makes you feel good and want to learn or teach, just to be in it. ____ ____

Comments:

Appendix C

Straight-Line Projections of Enrollments, Smalltown ISD

Grade	1993	1994	1995	1996	1997	1998	1999
K	25	22	24	19	28	23.6	24
1	23	25	25	32	24	25.8	24
2	22	18	22	22	28	22.4	26
3	27	20	23	24	21	23.0	22
4	26	23	19	21	32	24.2	23
5	29	17	27	21	20	22.8	24
6	36	27	18	21	19	24.2	23
Elem	188	152	158	160	172	166	166

Grade	1993	1994	1995	1996	1997	1998	1999
7	26	42	36	18	28	30.0	24
8	32	24	36	31	21	28.8	30
9	28	34	21	34	33	30.0	29
10	42	26	28	20	33	29.8	30
11	32	32	29	23	23	27.8	30
12	21	26	32	21	18	23.6	24
Sec	181	184	182	147	156	170.0	167

Total	369	336	340	307	328	336	333

Remedial Reading - 33   Music - 105
Special Education - 8   PE - 144

Room Utilization- Smalltown ISD

Elementary rooms, because of the size of furniture and equipment, can be used only for the grade and class for which they are assigned. Special Education rooms, and the secondary weight room, Ag and Ag shop, handball room, Science Lab, Boy's PE room, and Homemaking room are all special-purpose rooms which can't be used as general classrooms. The following rooms and schedules provide the only flexibility: (Student enrollment in parentheses)

Room	Period						
	1	2	3	4	5	6	7
1	(4)	(11)	(13)		(10)	(9)	(20)
2	(10)	(18)	(19)	(21)	(10)	(20)	
3	(4)	(10)		(16)	(9)	(1)	(7)
4	(20)	(6)	(13)	(24)	(16)	(18)	(25)
5	(18)	(7)	(16)	(14)	(16)	(5)	
6	(20)	(28)	(19)	(19)	(10)	(19)	(17)
7	(20)	(13)	(14)	(14)	(4)	(3)	
8	(4)	(15)	(8)	(5)	(18)	(11)	
(WRm1)							
9	(13)		(21)	(3)	(12)	(16)	(23)

There are only six unused period-rooms in the secondary section of the building, excluding the special purpose rooms, which gives a 90.47619 percent utilization. According to most experts, anything over 85 percent of utilization is acceptable. Special-purpose rooms were not figured into these usage percentages.

Appendix D

Final Presentation Outline
(For public presentation of final report)

Introductions (staff's and administrators) and who I am, where I'm from, and my qualifications for doing the study.

Task assigned by district:
Facilities adequacy
Facilities condition
Enrollment projections

Procedures:

Recommendations: (**Only** if requested by board of education)

Basic procedures will remain as agreed to in initial and subsequent planning sessions. All photographs, charts, narrative, and additional comments will remain the property of the Consultant, with the exception of those materials which are submitted as a part of the final report to the Board of Education.

Bibliography (Facilities)

American Association of School Administrators, National School Boards Association, and Council of Great City Schools, "The Maintenance Gap: Deferred Repair and Renovation in the Nation's Elementary and Secondary Schools", Arlington, VA, 1983

American Society of Heating, Refrigerating, and Air-Conditioning Engineers, "Ventilation for Acceptable Indoor Air Quality, Standard 62-1989", Atlanta, GA, 1989

Argonne National Laboratory, "Nationwide Survey of Energy Conservation in Public School Districts: Institutional, Organizational, and Technical Characteristics", Argonne, IL, 1987

"Building Education: How to Renew North America's Crumbling Schools", The American School Board Journal, The Executive Educator, and Service Master, Alexandria, VA, June, 1990

John Hancock Callender, "Time-Saver Standards for Architectural Design Data, 6th Edition", McGraw-Hill Book Co., New York, 1982

Carnegie Foundation for the Advancement of Teaching, "An Imperiled Generation: Saving Urban Schools", Washington, D.C., 1988

Committee on Architecture for Education, "Architecture-Related Concerns For New Learning Environments", American Institute of Architects, Washington, D.C., 1990

Joseph De Chiara, Lee E. Koppelman, "Time-Saver Standards for Site Planning", McGraw-Hill Book Co., New York, 1984

Nickalaus L. Engelhardt, "Complete Guide for Planning New Schools", Parker Publishing Co., Inc., New Nyack, N.Y., 1971

"Facilities For Special Education Services", Maryland State Department of Education for The Council for Exceptional Children, Reston, VA, 1979

Fenster, Larry C., "Maintenance Services: Keeping Them In-House or Contracting Them Out", School Business Affairs, July, 1991

Frier, Craig, "Confronting Deferred Maintenance", American School and University, April, 1991

"Guide for Planning Educational Facilities", Council of Educational Facilities Planners, International, Columbus, OH, 1976

Hensen, Shirley J., "Managing Indoor Air Quality", The Fairmont Press, Lilburn, GA, 1991

Harold D. Hauf and Joseph N. Boaz, "Architectural Graphic Standards", John Wiley and Sons, Inc., New York, 1970

John H. Holcomb, "A Guide to the Planning of Educational Facilities", Rafter "H" Publications, Granbury, TX, 1988

Don Koberg and Jim Bagnall, "The Universal Traveler", William Kaufmann, Inc., Los Altos, CA, 1976

Paul Laseau, "Graphic Problem Solving", CBI Publishing Co., Inc., Boston

"Life Safety Code", National Fire Protection Association, Quincy, MA, 1991

National Center for Educational Statistics, "The Condition of Education, 1990, Elementary and Secondary Education", U.S. Department of Education, Office of Educational Research and Improvement, Washington, D.C., 1991

"Opening All Doors: The ADA Videoconference", American Institute of Architects, Washington, D.C., 1992

"Schoolhouse in the RED", American Association of School Administrators, Arlington, VA, 1992

"Standard Building Code, 1982, As Amended (1983-84)", Southern Building Code Congress, International, Inc., Birmingham, AL, 1982

"Uniform Building Codes", International Conference of Building Officials, Whittier, CA, 1991

"Wolves at the Schoolhouse Door", Education Writers Association, Washington, D.C., 1989

About the Author

Dr. John H. Holcomb is Professor of Educational Administration, Tarleton State University, which is a part of the Texas A&M University System. He has served as a classroom teacher, coach, band director, elementary principal, junior high principal, senior high principal, district director of instruction and planning, state department supervisor of federal programs, and as superintendent of schools.

In addition, he has authored over three hundred newspaper and magazine articles, five books, and acts as consultant to school districts and others in the areas of management training, staff development, board and administration development, and conducts superintendent searches. He is founder and executive officer of the educational consulting firm, *Holcomb and Associates.*

Dr. Holcomb has served as president of his state's secondary principals and state superintendent's associations, respectively. He was founder and director of the Western States Coalition for Education as well as the Southeastern Colorado Educational Renewal Center. He has presented testimony in several state legislatures as well as both Houses of Congress.

He has served as a member of the Colorado state library board, as a member of the Colorado Equal Education Opportunities Commission, community hospital board member, urban renewal committee member, member of the Colorado Commission for the Aging, and as chairman of a local airport board.

He has served as a member of both state and national legislative committees representing local and state boards of education. He is a member of the Texas Association of School Board's Legislative Network, as well as the National School

Board Association's Legislative Network. He is a certified instructor in all 12 Standards required on Texas school board members. He serves as Executive Director of the Cross Timbers School Development Council, which represents an area containing almost 200 school districts.

Further, he is a four-time Fellow of the Kettering Foundation, four-time state representative to the American Association of School Administrator's Delegate Assembly, and served as chairman of the Colorado Federal Relations Commission. He was elected "Superintendent of the Year" by the National Community Education Association and was selected to serve on the AASA Architecture Jury. He is a retired lieutenant colonel, USAR.

In addition to his work in public and higher education, Dr. Holcomb has worked as consultant to a number of private-sector business and industries in the field of management and organization.